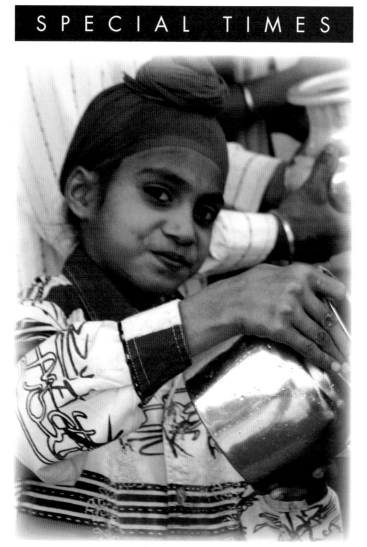

# A journey through life in
# Sikhism

Gerald Haigh
Consultant: Kanwaljit Kaur-Singh

# Contents

Published by A & C Black Publishers
Limited
36 Soho Square
London W1D 3QY
www.acblack.com

ISBN 978–1–4081–0434–7
Copyright © A & C Black Publishers
Limited 2009

Series concept: Suma Din
Series consultant: Lynne Broadbent
Created by Bookwork Ltd, Stroud, UK

A CIP catalogue record for this book is
available from the British Library.

A & C Black uses paper produced with
elemental chlorine-free pulp, harvested
from managed sustainable forests. It
is natural, renewable and recyclable.
The logging and manufacturing process
conform to the environmental regulations
of the country of origin.

Printed in China by Leo Paper Products

All the internet addresses given in this
book were correct at the time of going to
press. The author and publishers regret
any inconvenience caused if addresses
have changed or sites have ceased to
exist, but can accept no responsibility for
any such changes.

*6 A baby is a gift from God*

*12 Children eating in the Gurdwara*

*24 A bride and groom celebrating their marriage*

# How to use this book

Sikhism began in India, but there are now people all over the world who are **Sikhs**. This book tells you what it is like to be Sikh and about the special times, customs and beliefs of Sikhs.

## Finding your way

The pages in this book have been carefully planned to make it easy for you to find out about Sikhism. Here are two examples with explanations about the different features. Look at the Contents pages too, to read about each section.

Captions give a short description of a picture.

---

## Starting to wear the turban

Male Sikhs show their belief in their faith by wearing the **turban** – a long piece of cloth used to cover the head.

### Learning to tie the turban

Boys start to wear the turban when they are old enough to tie it, usually when they are about 11 years old. Before this, they wear their hair tied on top of their head in a topknot called a jura. Children learn how to tie the turban from people at the Gurdwara. Then they practise at home.

When Sikh children are ready to wear the turban, they have a turban-tying ceremony at the Gurdwara. Family and friends are invited. A Granthi or Sikh elder ties the child's turban in the ceremony and everyone celebrates with Langar afterwards.

*A young boy with his hair tied in a jura and covered with a clean cloth called a ramal.*

Jaskaran is 16. He explains what it means to him to wear a turban.

Every morning I spend 20 minutes combing my hair and tying my turban. I take great pride in doing it neatly so that it looks smart. As I do so, I remember the last human Guru, Guru Gobind Singh, who told us to wear the turban. I feel close to him and to God. For me, putting on my turban is a kind of prayer, and I am showing what I believe by wearing it.

Case studies give a Sikh person's own experience of a custom described in the section.

Comments give additional information about something specific in a picture.

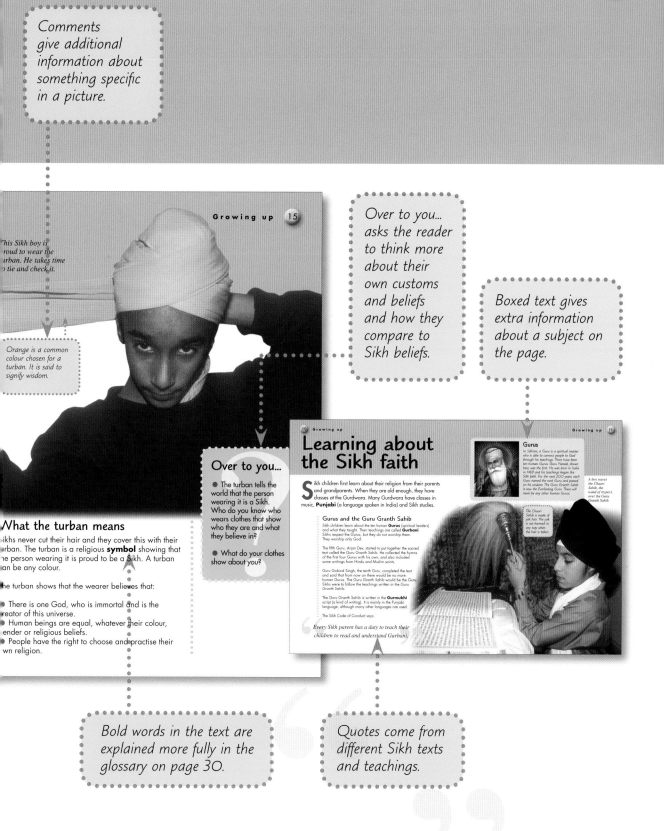

This Sikh boy is proud to wear the turban. He takes time to tie and check it.

Orange is a common colour chosen for a turban. It is said to signify wisdom.

Over to you... asks the reader to think more about their own customs and beliefs and how they compare to Sikh beliefs.

Boxed text gives extra information about a subject on the page.

## Over to you...

● The turban tells the world that the person wearing it is a Sikh. Who do you know who wears clothes that show who they are and what they believe in?

● What do your clothes show about you?

## What the turban means

Sikhs never cut their hair and they cover this with their turban. The turban is a religious **symbol** showing that the person wearing it is proud to be a Sikh. A turban can be any colour.

The turban shows that the wearer believes that:

● There is one God, who is immortal and is the creator of this universe.
● Human beings are equal, whatever their colour, gender or religious beliefs.
● People have the right to choose and practise their own religion.

# Learning about the Sikh faith

Sikh children first learn about their religion from their parents and grandparents. When they are old enough, they have classes at the Gurdwara. Many Gurdwara have classes in music, **Punjabi** (a language spoken in India) and Sikh studies.

### Gurus and the Guru Granth Sahib

Sikh children learn about the ten human **Gurus** (spiritual leaders) and what they taught. Their teachings are called **Gurbani**. Sikhs respect the Gurus, but they do not worship them. They worship only God.

The fifth Guru, Arjan Dev, started to put together the sacred text called the Guru Granth Sahib. He collected the hymns of the first four Gurus with his own, and also included some writings from Hindu and Muslim saints.

Guru Gobind Singh, the tenth Guru, completed the text and said that from now on there would be no more human Gurus. The Guru Granth Sahib would be the Guru. Sikhs were to follow the teachings written in the Guru Granth Sahib.

The Guru Granth Sahib is written in the **Gurmukhi** script (a kind of writing). It is mainly in the Punjabi language, although many other languages are used.

The Sikh Code of Conduct says:

*Every Sikh parent has a duty to teach their children to read and understand Gurbani.*

### Gurus

In Sikhism, a Guru is a spiritual master who is able to connect people to God through his teachings. There have been ten human Gurus. Guru Nanak, shown here, was the first. He was born in India in 1469 and his teachings began the Sikh faith. For the next 200 years, each Guru named the next Guru and passed on his wisdom. The Guru Granth Sahib is now the Everlasting Guru. There will never be any other human Gurus.

A boy waves the Chauri Sahib, the wand of respect, over the Guru Granth Sahib.

The Chauri Sahib is made of yak hair. The yak is not harmed in any way when the hair is taken.

Bold words in the text are explained more fully in the glossary on page 30.

Quotes come from different Sikh texts and teachings.

# A new member of the family

The birth of a baby is an exciting and happy time for the family. For Sikh families, it's also a **spiritual** time. The baby is a new member of the Sikh community.

## Blessing a baby

A Sikh child is a gift from God, welcomed with prayer and thankfulness. From the moment a child is born, the parents follow the instructions set out in the **Sikh Code of Conduct** (rules that tell Sikhs how to live their lives) and the **Guru Granth Sahib** (the collection of Sikh scriptures).

An important person from the **Gurdwara** (the Sikh place of worship) might be invited to visit the baby at home. This person, called a **Granthi**, says a prayer and stirs water and sugar in an iron bowl to make holy water called **Amrit**. The Granthi puts a drop of Amrit on the baby's tongue and the mother drinks the rest. This blessing reminds everyone of the importance of God in their lives.

## The soul

Sikhs believe that a baby's **soul** went through many different lives before it entered the human form. When each life ended, the soul was born again into a different body until it was born into a human body. Sikhs believe that the human is the highest life form created by God. Therefore, when a human dies, the soul can finally reach God.

The Guru Granth Sahib says:

" *Through 8.4 million* **incarnations** *you have wandered, to obtain this rare and precious human life.* "

A Sikh mother and her new baby in London. As soon as she is able, the mother will take her baby to the Gurdwara. There she will be joined by family and friends.

# Choosing a name for a baby

**S**ikh babies are given their names during a ceremony in the presence of the Guru Granth Sahib. Some families may decide to have the naming ceremony at home. Many families have the ceremony at the Gurdwara.

*A Granthi is reading from the Guru Granth Sahib, which was opened at a random page.*

## The first letter

Parents use the Guru Granth Sahib to help them to choose a name. A Granthi opens the Guru Granth Sahib at random. The first letter of the first prayer on the left-hand page will be the first letter of the baby's name. For example, if the prayer begins with a J, the baby might be called Jaspreet, which means 'the love of hymns'. Sometimes the whole word is used if it has a good meaning.

## Sikh names

Sikhs do not use different names for girls and boys. Jaspreet, Arjan, Ranjeet or any other Sikh name can be used for either a girl or a boy. This reminds Sikhs that all names are spiritual and that men and women are equal before God.

Girls have the special Sikh surname Kaur, meaning 'princess', added to their name. Boys have the special Sikh surname Singh, meaning 'lion', added to their name. So a girl with the name Jaspreet would be called Jaspreet Kaur and a boy would be called Jaspreet Singh. These names show that a person is proud to be a Sikh and is faithful to God.

Ranjeet is 10 years old. He lives in London. His new baby sister has just been born.

Guess what! We have a new baby in our house. She hasn't got a name yet, but we call her Rani. It means 'little princess' and it shows how precious she is to us. She'll get her proper name when we pray at the Gurdwara. People have been bringing us presents to celebrate, and my dad gave all our neighbours, family and friends sweets because it's such a happy time.

## Over to you...

● Does your name have a special meaning?

● How was your name chosen?

*A Sikh child welcomes a new baby into his family. Children are encouraged to help to look after younger ones.*

# Learning about the Sikh faith

Sikh children first learn about their religion from their parents and grandparents. When they are old enough, they have classes at the Gurdwara. Many Gurdwara have classes in music, **Punjabi** (a language spoken in India) and Sikh studies.

## Gurus and the Guru Granth Sahib

Sikh children learn about the ten human **Gurus** (spiritual leaders) and what they taught. Their teachings are called **Gurbani**. Sikhs respect the Gurus, but they do not worship them. They worship only God.

The fifth Guru, Arjan Dev, started to put together the sacred text called the Guru Granth Sahib. He collected the hymns of the first four Gurus with his own, and also included some writings from Hindu and Muslim saints.

Guru Gobind Singh, the tenth Guru, completed the text and said that from now on there would be no more human Gurus. The Guru Granth Sahib would be the Guru. Sikhs were to follow the teachings written in the Guru Granth Sahib.

The Guru Granth Sahib is written in the **Gurmukhi** script (a kind of writing). It is mainly in the Punjabi language, although many other languages are used.

The Sikh Code of Conduct says:

*Every Sikh parent has a duty to teach their children to read and understand Gurbani.*

# Gurus

In Sikhism, a Guru is a spiritual master who is able to connect people to God through his teachings. There have been ten human Gurus. Guru Nanak, shown here, was the first. He was born in India in 1469 and his teachings began the Sikh faith. For the next 200 years, each Guru named the next Guru and passed on his wisdom. The Guru Granth Sahib is now the Everlasting Guru. There will never be any other human Gurus.

*A boy waves the Chauri Sahib, the wand of respect, over the Guru Granth Sahib.*

The Chauri Sahib is made of yak hair. The yak is not harmed in any way when the hair is taken.

# Worshipping at the Gurdwara

**T**he Gurdwara is very important. It is a place for worship, for meeting and for sharing meals. It is the centre of a Sikh community and there is always something happening there.

*Sikh musicians called ragis sing Gurbani, the Gurus' words, during worship at a Gurdwara in the UK.*

## Inside the Gurdwara

Everyone sits on the floor in the prayer hall in the Gurdwara. This tells Sikhs that God accepts everyone equally. There is a bowl of **Karah Parshad**, a sweet-tasting food. Anyone who visits the prayer hall is given a small amount to eat. This makes them all equal and reminds them of the importance of sharing.

There is always music in the Gurdwara. Sikhs love to sing hymns. The Guru Granth Sahib has 1,430 pages of hymns.

## Over to you...

● What places of worship have you visited? What things were the same as in a Gurdwara? What things were different?

● Is eating a special time for you and your family? What sort of special meals does your family share?

## Eating together

Sikhs believe that food is a gift from God and a sign of His love.

At the end of a service in the Gurdwara, everyone eats together. The name of the meal that everyone shares is called the **Langar**. The place where it is eaten is also called the Langar. It is sometimes called 'the Gurus' kitchen'. Everyone sits on the floor and shares the same food. Eating together is a sign of equality. No one is ever turned away. Sikhs welcome everyone, not just Sikhs.

The Sikh Code of Conduct says:

*A Sikh father shares Langar in a Gurdwara in the UK with his children and their friends.*

" *Do not eat on your own, always try to share with others.* "

# Starting to wear the turban

**M**ale Sikhs show their belief in their faith by wearing the **turban** – a long piece of cloth used to cover the head.

*A young boy with his hair tied in a jura and covered with a clean cloth called a ramal.*

### Learning to tie the turban

Boys start to wear the turban when they are old enough to tie it, usually when they are about 11 years old. Before this, they wear their hair tied on top of their head in a topknot called a jura. Children learn how to tie the turban from people at the Gurdwara. Then they practise at home.

When Sikh children are ready to wear the turban, they have a turban-tying ceremony at the Gurdwara. Family and friends are invited. A Granthi or Sikh elder ties the child's turban in the ceremony and everyone celebrates with Langar afterwards.

Jaskaran is 16. He explains what it means to him to wear a turban.

Every morning I spend 20 minutes combing my hair and tying my turban. I take great pride in doing it neatly so that it looks smart. As I do so, I remember the last human Guru, Guru Gobind Singh, who told us to wear the turban. I feel close to him and to God. For me, putting on my turban is a kind of prayer, and I am showing what I believe by wearing it.

*This Sikh boy is proud to wear the turban. He takes time to tie and check it.*

*Orange is a common colour chosen for a turban. It is said to signify wisdom.*

## What the turban means

Sikhs never cut their hair and they cover this with their turban. The turban is a religious **symbol** showing that the person wearing it is proud to be a Sikh. A turban can be any colour.

The turban shows that the wearer believes that:

● There is one God, who is immortal and is the creator of this universe.
● Human beings are equal, whatever their colour, gender or religious beliefs.
● People have the right to choose and practise their own religion.

## Over to you...

● The turban tells the world that the person wearing it is a Sikh. Who do you know who wears clothes that show who they are and what they believe in?

● What do your clothes show about you?

# A full member of the faith

**W**hen a Sikh becomes a teenager, he or she can decide to become a full member of the faith. A Sikh who decides to do this takes part in a ceremony called taking Amrit.

## Amrit ceremony

Taking Amrit is a very important ceremony in a Sikh's life. It takes place in private in the Gurdwara. Five Sikhs, called the Panj Piare, who have already taken Amrit, lead the ceremony. They represent the first five Sikhs who took Amrit with Guru Gobind Singh.

Amrit is a special mixture of sugar crystals and water. It is stirred in an iron bowl with a **Khanda** (double-edged sword) and prayers are said. Sikhs believe that the prayers make the Amrit very spiritual.

*Men and women of all ages wait for the Amrit ceremony to begin in a Gurdwara in London. The five people in yellow robes are the Panj Piare.*

Gurvinda is 18 and lives in the USA. He remembers when he took Amrit.

Taking Amrit was like starting a whole new life. It really felt like I had woken up after hundreds of years and now I could appreciate this life. I was proud to have become part of something much bigger and more spiritual. I felt connected to all the other Sikhs who had chosen to live a pure life.

# Becoming a full member of Sikhism

The person taking Amrit drinks the sweet sugar water five times, to help them speak sweetly and kindly. The Amrit is sprinkled into their eyes to help them see that all people are equal. Finally, it is sprinkled on their head to help them to think with an open mind and not be prejudiced against other people and faiths.

After the Amrit ceremony, a Sikh is given guidelines, which they promise to follow for the rest of their lives. This makes them a member of the **Khalsa**, the community of people who have chosen to live a pure life close to God. They must:

- Never cut their hair
- Wear the **Five Ks** (see page 18)
- Never drink or smoke tobacco
- Lead a faithful family life
- Worship God through prayers written by the Gurus.

*The Panj Piare prepare the Amrit. They sit in a semi-circle with their fingertips on the bowl. The head Piare stirs the mixture with a Khanda.*

# How Sikhs show their beliefs

Sikhs believe that there is one God who is eternal and is everywhere. Guru Gobind Singh ordered Sikhs to show their commitment to their beliefs and to God through five symbols.

*The Khanda emblem. The double-edged sword has a circle around it showing that God has no beginning and no end. On each side there is a single-edged sword: one for God's rules and one for the rules we obey here on Earth.*

## The Five Ks

The words for these five symbols all begin with the letter K, so the symbols have always been known as the Five Ks. They are worn by men and women.

● Kesh – uncut hair and beard. This shows respect for the way God created us. Men cover their hair with a turban. Women usually tie their hair in a bun and cover it with a chunni (scarf) in the Gurdwara.
● Kangha – wooden comb to keep the hair tidy and clean. It is a sign of discipline and cleanliness.
● Kachera – special cotton shorts. They symbolise modesty and self-respect.
● Kara – a steel or iron bangle. It is not worn as jewellery but as a symbol to remind Sikhs of their duty to do right.
● Kirpan – a sword. This is a symbol of God's supreme power and reminds Sikhs of their duty to defend the weak.

## The Khanda

Outside every Gurdwara hangs a flag with a design called the Khanda. The Khanda design has a double-edged sword (also called a Khanda) in the middle to represent God's power as creator.

*God was True before time began and is True throughout the ages.*

After combing his hair, the man will keep the Kangha in his hair, under his turban.

The Kara is a reminder that God, like the bangle, has neither beginning nor end.

A Sikh man combs his hair before tying his turban. This is done every day.

# Living as an adult Sikh

**L**iving a good and honest life is an important part of being a Sikh. Adult Sikhs try to follow the example of the Gurus by living their lives in a way that honours their beliefs and values.

*This Sikh couple work together to run a local post office. They work hard as equal partners to earn their living.*

## Faith in everyday life

Sikhism teaches that a Sikh should follow three rules.

● Nam Japna – to read the Guru Granth Sahib and follow its teachings. Sikhs pray, **meditate** and read the Guru Granth Sahib as often as possible. The Mool Mantra is an important verse in the Guru Granth Sahib. Sikhs say it to themselves or out loud. It starts, "There is only one God, who is the truth and the creator without fear and hate, and who is beyond time and birth and death."

● Kirat Karna – to work hard to earn an honest living. When it is time to find a job, a faithful Sikh will take one that is honest and does not damage the work or lives of others. Sikhs also try hard to be of service to others and to respect people of all backgrounds and beliefs.

● Vand Chhakna – to share earnings with the less fortunate. Sikhs who earn a lot of money use it to make others happy. Even Sikhs who earn only small wages will always give some money to **charity**.

> *Blessed is the godly person and the riches they possess because they can be used for charitable purposes and to give happiness.*

Darshan Singh is 32 and lives in Leeds, England. He talks about his life and work.

I'm a bus driver and I'm proud of my work. I serve the public, always doing my best for the safety and comfort of my passengers. It is honest work and I do it well. Sometimes, when I'm waiting at the terminus, I pray. My employers understand my faith and allow me to wear my turban at work. I don't earn much money, but I always give some to charity. God has given me a good life, and I am thankful.

*Sikhs wear the turban to work. Where possible, they wear a turban to match their uniform, such as that of a doorman (above) and a policeman (left).*

# Deciding to get engaged

A Sikh wedding is not only the joining of two people, but also the joining of two families. This means the opinion of a young Sikh's family is important when choosing a husband or wife.

## Two families

When young Sikhs fall in love and want to get married, their families get to know each other too. They want to agree that the marriage is a good idea. As a couple become closer, the families visit each other and have meals together. Then the couple get engaged in a ceremony at the Gurdwara.

Sometimes a family helps to choose a husband or wife for a daughter or son. If the couple like each other, they agree to get engaged.

*Friends sing in the presence of the Guru Granth Sahib.*

Jaswant Singh is 40 years old and lives in Scotland. He describes how he met his wife.

When I started to earn money, I discussed marriage with my parents. They asked family and friends if they knew any young women for me. One in particular seemed suitable and I must have seemed suitable to her! We had to agree on this because Sikh marriages are between equals. We fell in love and got engaged and have been together for 20 years now. We know we and our families did exactly the right thing.

# The engagement ceremony

When a couple agree to get engaged, they might have a party. This can be held at the boy or girl's home, or in the Gurdwara. The **shabads** (hymns) are sung in the presence of the Guru Granth Sahib, and families and friends ask for God's blessings. Gifts of jewellery and clothes are exchanged.

Sometimes a Kirpan is given to remind the engaged person of the importance of the Five Ks.

*A girl's friends sing hymns suitable for happy occasions, to ask for God's blessing on her engagement ceremony.*

# Celebrating a Sikh wedding

A Sikh wedding is a joyous and festive occasion. It is called Anand Karaj, which means 'Ceremony of Bliss'. Everyone enjoys Langar together afterwards in the Langar Hall.

*A couple sit before the Guru Granth Sahib to listen to the Laavan during their wedding in the UK.*

*The bride and groom hold a scarf, which symbolises that they are joined together.*

## The wedding ceremony

A Sikh wedding takes place at the bride's local Gurdwara. As the groom's relatives and friends arrive, the bride's family greets them and offers food.

The ceremony takes place in the main hall. The Granthi starts by reading the shabad (hymn) linking the couple spiritually. The father of the bride then takes a scarf from the groom's shoulder and places one end in his daughter's hand. This links the couple together.

The Granthi then recites four special verses called the **Laavan**. The verses remind the couple of their responsibilities to God, to each other and to their fellow human beings.

At the end of each verse, the couple bow before the Guru Granth Sahib and walk around it holding the scarf firmly in their hands. Walking around the Guru Granth Sahib shows that they accept that its holy teachings are at the centre of their lives.

## Over to you...

● Are the Laavan similar to the wedding promises of other religions?

● Which Sikh marriage promises do you think are the most important?

# The Laavan

The verses of the Laavan are sung as well as read out loud.

● First Laav – the couple's marriage is in God's name and their lives are to be lived as God would want.

● Second Laav – the couple must be respectful and loving to each other. They must not be selfish or thoughtless. They are like one person together.

● Third Laav – the couple, in their love and togetherness, have become free from everyday thoughts and feelings. For the moment, their only thoughts are of each other and of God.

● Fourth Laav – the couple have also become one with God.

*A bride and groom are given gifts of money to help them to start a new home. This is a Punjabi cultural custom, not a religious requirement.*

# Respecting older people

Older people are a vital part of the Sikh community. They are highly valued and treated with great respect. This respect begins in the family, which is very important in Sikhism.

## The wisdom of grandparents

Traditionally, Sikhs live with three generations in the home – grandparents, parents and children. Grandparents are able to give advice and use their experience and wisdom to benefit the whole family. The relationship between grandparents and children is seen as particularly important. Grandparents may spend a lot of time with the children if parents are working, and children can often relate in a special way to them and gain comfort and support from them.

## Retired Sikhs

The respect that Sikhs have for older people means that retired Sikhs are regarded as valued and experienced advisors. They may continue to use the skills they had in their jobs, or they may use their lifetime of wisdom and knowledge to help people to solve problems in their lives. They may do this at the Gurdwara, or in their own homes or both.

Hardeep Kaur is 12 years old. She talks about her Babaji – her grandfather.

Babaji lives in our house and is very special. He tells me lots of stories about the Punjab (an area of India) and about my mother when she was young. He is respected and gives advice to many young men and women. Lots of people visit him at home. Sometimes he goes to the Gurdwara to give people advice. Babaji doesn't have much money to give to others but he does have lots of time to give. I'm proud that he is my Babaji.

A retired Sikh says a prayer at the Gurdwara. He helps to prepare Langar at the Gurdwara and explains the Sikh faith to visitors.

# When someone we love dies

**A**ll things that are born will also die. Although it is sad when a loved one dies, Sikhs believe it is God's will. They believe that death is not an end, but is part of a journey.

## Reaching God

Sikhs believe that when a person dies, their soul should reach God. This depends on how they have lived their life. If they have followed the teachings of the Gurus, then their soul will most certainly reach God.

However, if a person has lived by poor moral and spiritual standards, their soul may come back in another form. It may be animal or human and this is God's choice. Once the soul comes back in human form again, there is another chance to reach God. Guru Nanak said that human life is a precious gift from God and must not be wasted.

## A Sikh funeral

When Sikhs die, they are not buried. Their family has a **cremation** in which the dead body is burnt until it turns into ashes. If possible, the person's ashes are scattered at a special Gurdwara in India called Kiratpur Sahib. This is where the ashes of some of the Gurus were scattered.

The family then reads the Guru Granth Sahib. Some families have Akhand Path, when they read the whole Guru Granth Sahib, which takes 48 hours. Each person reads for two hours at a time. The words comfort those who read them and those who listen.

*A boy takes his turn at the family's reading of the Guru Granth Sahib after the death of a relative.*

Sandeep is 11. She lives in London.
She remembers her grandfather's funeral.

I have a wonderful memory of travelling to India with my grandfather's ashes. We were taking his ashes in a special urn back to his homeland. As we got off the plane, I remember my mother saying, "Home again, Father. One day we will come home too, to be with you."

## Over to you...

● What do you think happens when a person dies?

● Have you ever been to a funeral? How was it similar to and different from a Sikh funeral?

Young Sikh boys and girls are taught to read the Guru Granth Sahib so that they can understand its teachings.

# Glossary and more information

**Amrit** Holy water consisting of sugar crystals dissolved in water. It is used in religious ceremonies.

**charity** Help given out voluntarily. Also, an organisation set up to help and protect people, animals or the environment.

**cremation** A funeral in which a dead body is burnt until it turns to ashes.

**Five Ks** The five symbols of the *Sikh* faith.

**Granthi** A person who reads the *Guru Granth Sahib*. Sometimes, a full-time person in the *Gurdwara*.

**Gurbani** The teachings of the *Gurus*.

**Gurdwara** The *Sikh* place of worship. It means 'The *Guru's* door'.

**Gurmukhi** The written form of *Punjabi* used in the *Guru Granth Sahib*.

**Guru** A *spiritual* master. There were ten human Gurus.

**Guru Granth Sahib** The present and Everlasting *Guru*. It contains the written, sacred teachings that *Sikhs* must follow.

**incarnation** A physical form for a *soul*, such as a human or an animal. *Sikhs* believe the soul goes through many incarnations.

**Karah Parshad** A mixture of butter, flour, water and sugar tasted by all who worship or visit the *Gurdwara*. It shows equality of all.

**Khalsa** The community of commited *Sikhs* who have taken *Amrit*. It means 'Pure Ones'.

**Khanda** A double-edged sword. Also the design used as the *Sikh* emblem.

**Laavan** Four wedding verses composed by *Guru* Ram Das, the Fourth Guru.

**Langar** Food served in the *Gurdwara*. Also, the place where this food is served.

**meditate** To concentrate deeply.

**Punjabi** A language spoken in the Punjab area of India, where there are many *Sikhs*.

**shabad** A hymn sung at a religious ceremony. The words of the shabads were written or spoken by the *Gurus*.

**Sikh** Someone who follows the religion of Sikhism, founded by *Guru* Nanak in the 15th century, in the Punjab area of India.

**Sikh Code of Conduct** A set of rules drawn up in modern times that tell *Sikhs* how they should live their lives.

**soul** The *spiritual* part of a person, which lives in the body.

**spiritual** Relating to a religious belief.

**symbol** A real thing that stands for an idea or another thing.

**turban** The head covering worn by *Sikhs* as a sign of commitment to their faith.

# Things to do

Invite a member of the local Sikh community to come and talk to your class about their faith.

Find out where your nearest Gurdwara is. There is a list of UK Gurdwaras on the webpage www.boss-uk.org/gurdwara. Ask your teacher to help you arrange a visit.

Find out about the life and work of the ten human Gurus.

Find out what happened on Baisakhi day on 30 March 1699. Why is this day so important to Sikhs? Have a look at the website www.baisakhifestival.com

What situations can you think of, when it could be difficult for Sikhs to insist on wearing the Five Ks? Discuss in your class how a Sikh could deal with these situations.

Sikhs believe it is very important that they are prepared to accept the consequences of their own actions. The Guru Granth Sahib says: "O foolish mind! Why do you grumble when you are rewarded according to your own actions?" What do you think about this?

# More information

Find out more about Sikhism on these wesbites or from the Network of Sikh Organisations.

## Websites

**www.info-sikh.com**
Find out lots about the history and beliefs of Sikhism on this website. It has loads of information about the Gurus in particular.

**www.bbc.co.uk/religion/religions/sikhism**
This BBC website about Sikhism has sections on topics such as rituals, customs, history, holy days and people.

**www.reonline.org.uk**
This website has separate sections for teachers and children of different ages. It has links to other useful websites where you can find out about Sikhism and other religions.

**www.sikhs.org**
Sections on this easy-to-use website include information on the origin and development of Sikhism, the Sikh way of life and Sikh scriptures. There is also a section of 'resources', which contains a glossary of Sikh terms, a list of Sikh names and their meanings and much more.

## Organisations

**Network of Sikh Organisations**
Suite 405, Highland House
165 The Broadway
Wimbledon
SW19 1NE
Tel: 020 8544 8037
www.nsouk.co.uk

# Index

## Picture credits

The publisher would like to thank the following for their kind permission to reproduce their photographs.

Position key: c=centre; b=bottom; t=top; l=left; r=right

1c: G B Mukherji/World Relgions Photo Library;
3cr: Christine Osborne/World Religions Photo Library;
3tr: Christine Osborne/World Relgions Photo Library;
3br: Christine Osborne/World Religions Photo Library;
7c: Christine Osborne/World Religions Photo Library;
8cl: Christine Osborne/World Religions Photo Library;

9c: Rohit Seth/Shutterstock; 9tl: Christine Osborne/World Religions Photo Library; 11tl: Christine Osborne/World Religions Photo Library; 11bc: Christine Osborne/World Religions Photo Library; 12bc: Christine Osborne/World Religions Photo Library; 13c: Christine Osborne/World Religions Photo Library; 14bl: Christine Osborne/World Religions Photo Library; 14cl: G B Mukherji/World Religions Photo Library; 15tc: Christine Osborne/World Religions Photo Library; 16bc: Christine Osborne/World Religions Photo Library; 17tl: Vikram Raghuvanshi/iStockphoto; 17c: Paul Gapper/World Religions Photo Library; 18cl: Ajmone Tristano/Shutterstock; 19c: Christine Osborne/World Religions Photo Library; 20bl: Christine Osborne/World

Religions Photo Library; 21tl: Vikram Raghuvanshi/iStockphoto; 21cr: Christine Osborne/World Religions Photo Library; 21bc: Christine Osborne/World Religions Photo Library; 22bl: Vikram Raghuvanshi/iStockphoto; 23bc: Claire Stout/World Religions Photo Library; 24cl: Christine Osborne/World Religions Photo Library; 24bc: Christine Osborne/World Religions Photo Library; 25c: Christine Osborne/World Religions Photo Library; 26bl: Paul Gapper/World Religions Photo Library; 27c: Christine Osborne/World Religions Photo Library; 29cr: Christine Osborne/World Religions Photo Library; 29tl: Christine Osborne/World Religions Photo Library

Cover photograph: © Paul Doyle/Alamy